Anonymous

Excell's Anthems for the Choir

Consisting of solos, duets, trios, quartetts [sic], choruses, etc.

Anonymous

Excell's Anthems for the Choir
Consisting of solos, duets, trios, quartetts [sic], choruses, etc.

ISBN/EAN: 9783337297794

Printed in Europe, USA, Canada, Australia, Japan

Cover: Foto ©Thomas Meinert / pixelio.de

More available books at **www.hansebooks.com**

"Sing unto the Lord.

Excell's Anthems

FOR THE CHOIR.

Consisting of

Solos, Duets, Trios, Quartetts, Choruses

ETC., ETC.

WRITTEN BY A LARGE LIST OF ABLE COMPOSERS.

PUBLISHER.
LAKESIDE BUILDING, E. O. EXCELL, CHICAGO, ILLINOIS.

COPYRIGHT, 1888, BY E. O. EXCELL.

CONTENTS.
VOL. II.

Angels, ever bright and fair	Handel.	261
As panteth the hart	Davis.	246
Come, Holy Spirit	Beirly.	341
Come, thou fount	Harrison.	304
Consider the lilies	Excell.	185
Departed friends	Ryder.	294
Evening Hymn	Excell.	364
From every stormy wind that blows	Wilder.	355
Give Alms (*Solo Anon, Quartet*)	Beirly.	360
Glory to God in the highest	Danks.	313
Gracious Spirit, love divine	Lewis.	205
Hearken, O Lord	Mackenzie.	334
He giveth his beloved sleep	Danks.	255
I was glad	Dungan.	222
I will extol thee	Excell.	320
I will lift up mine eyes	McAllister.	240
I will praise thee	O'Kane.	276
Jesus, lover of my soul	Excell.	258
Lift up your heads, O ye gates	Ogden.	217
Nearer, my God, to thee	Sweney.	200
O be joyful	Fairbank.	285
O God, my heart is fixed	Beirly.	266
One sweetly solemn thought	Ambrose.	356
O Paradise, O Paradise	Beirly.	306
O praise the Lord	Sweney.	348
Praise the Lord, O Jerusalem	Danks.	228
Praise ye the Lord	Scott.	297
Savior, Source of ev'ry blessing	Beirly.	194
Sun of my soul	Hall.	234
The Lord is merciful	Scott.	252
The nations who are saved	Whittington.	308
There is a fountain fill'd with blood	Beirly.	328
Trust in the Lord and do good	Scott.	272
Wake the song of jubilee	Excell.	210

EXCELL'S ANTHEMS.

VOL. II.

CONSIDER THE LILIES.

E. O. EXCELL.

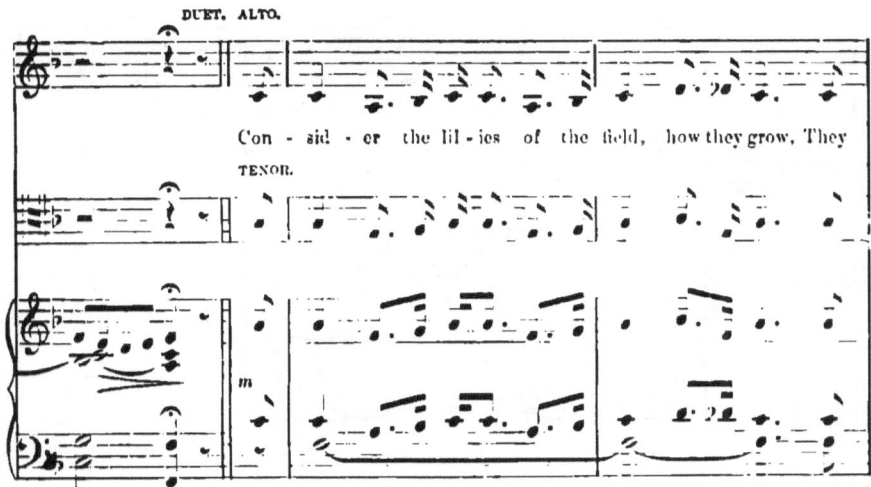

188   CONSIDER THE LILIES. CONTINUED.

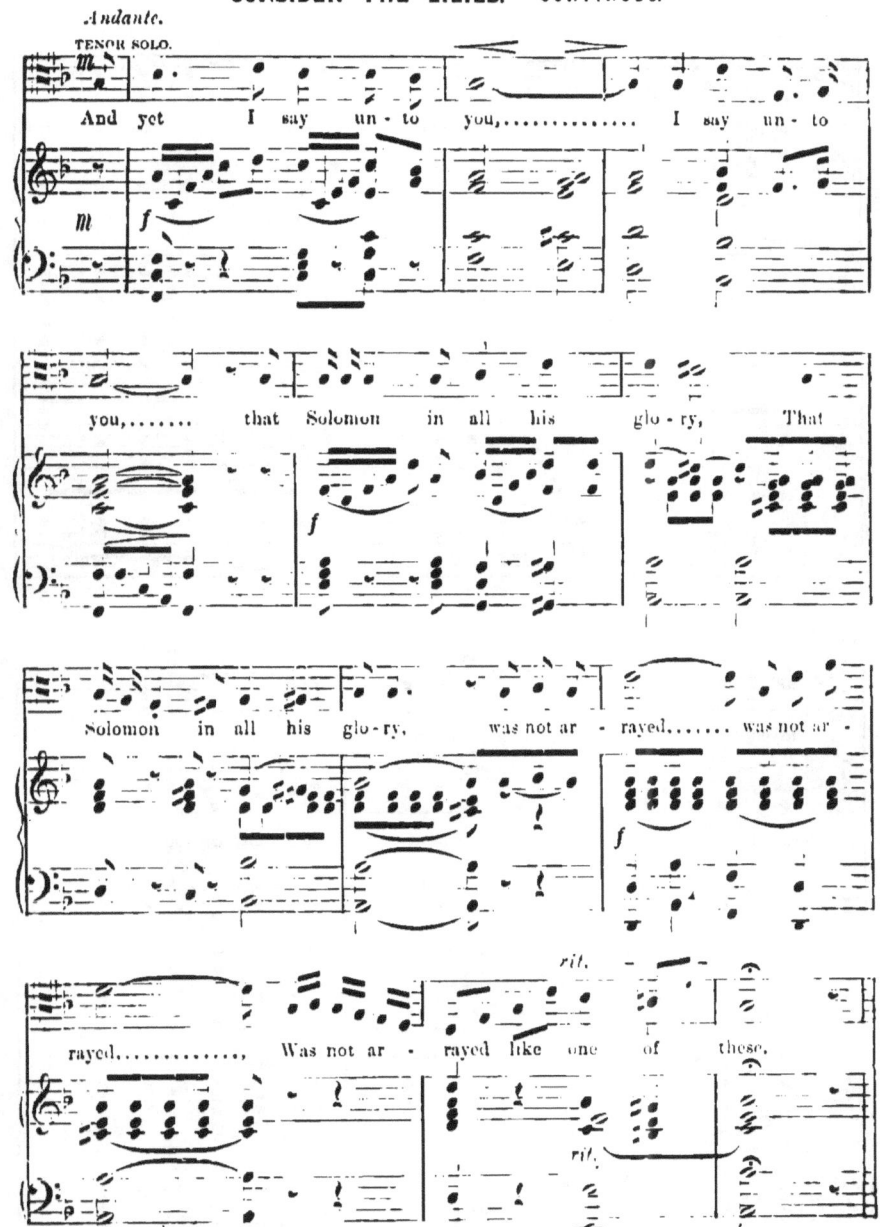

CONSIDER THE LILIES. CONTINUED.

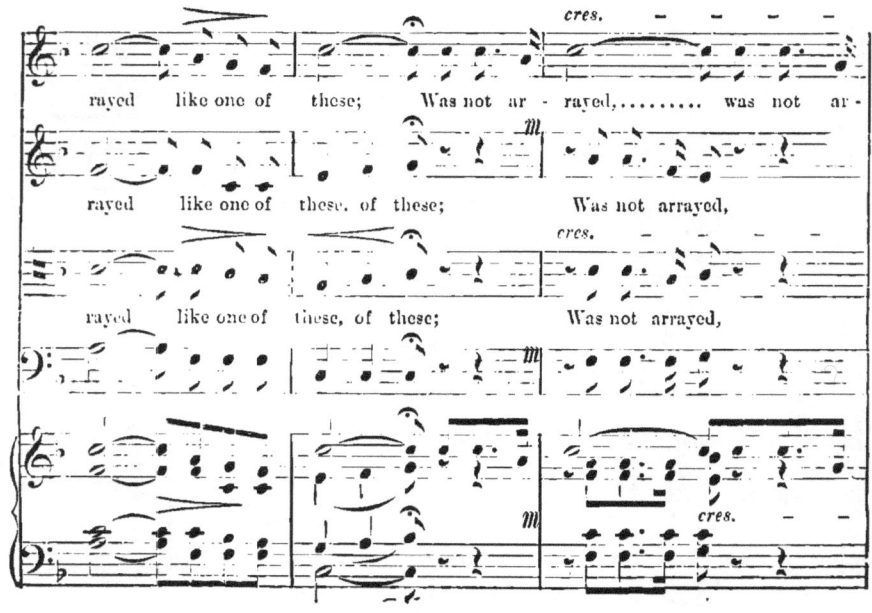

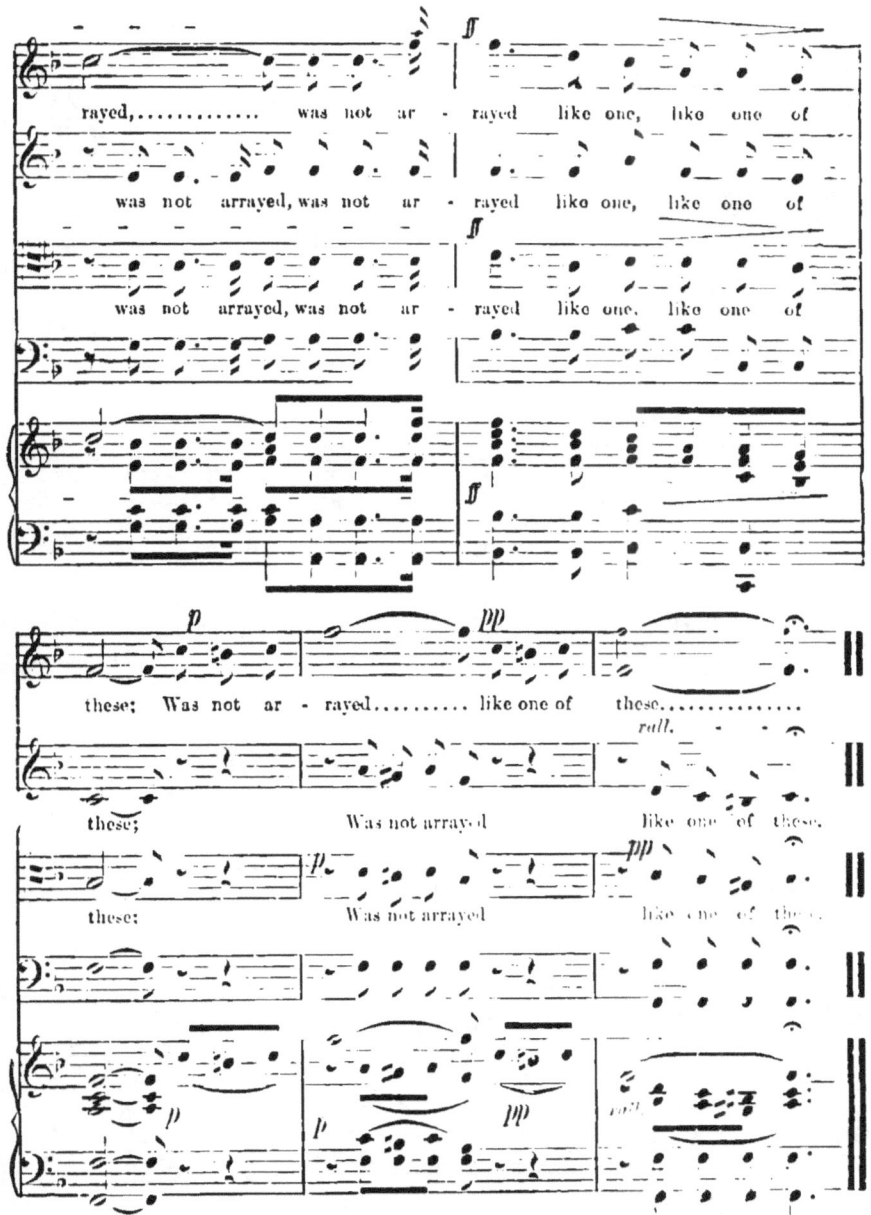

194. SAVIOR, SOURCE OF EV'RY BLESSING.

A. BEIRLY.

Lyrics: Savior, source of ev'ry blessing, Tune my heart to grateful lays; Streams of mercy, never ceasing, Call for songs of loudest praise.

Copyright, 1888, by E. O. Excell.

SAVIOR, SOURCE OF EV'RY BLESSING. CONTINUED.

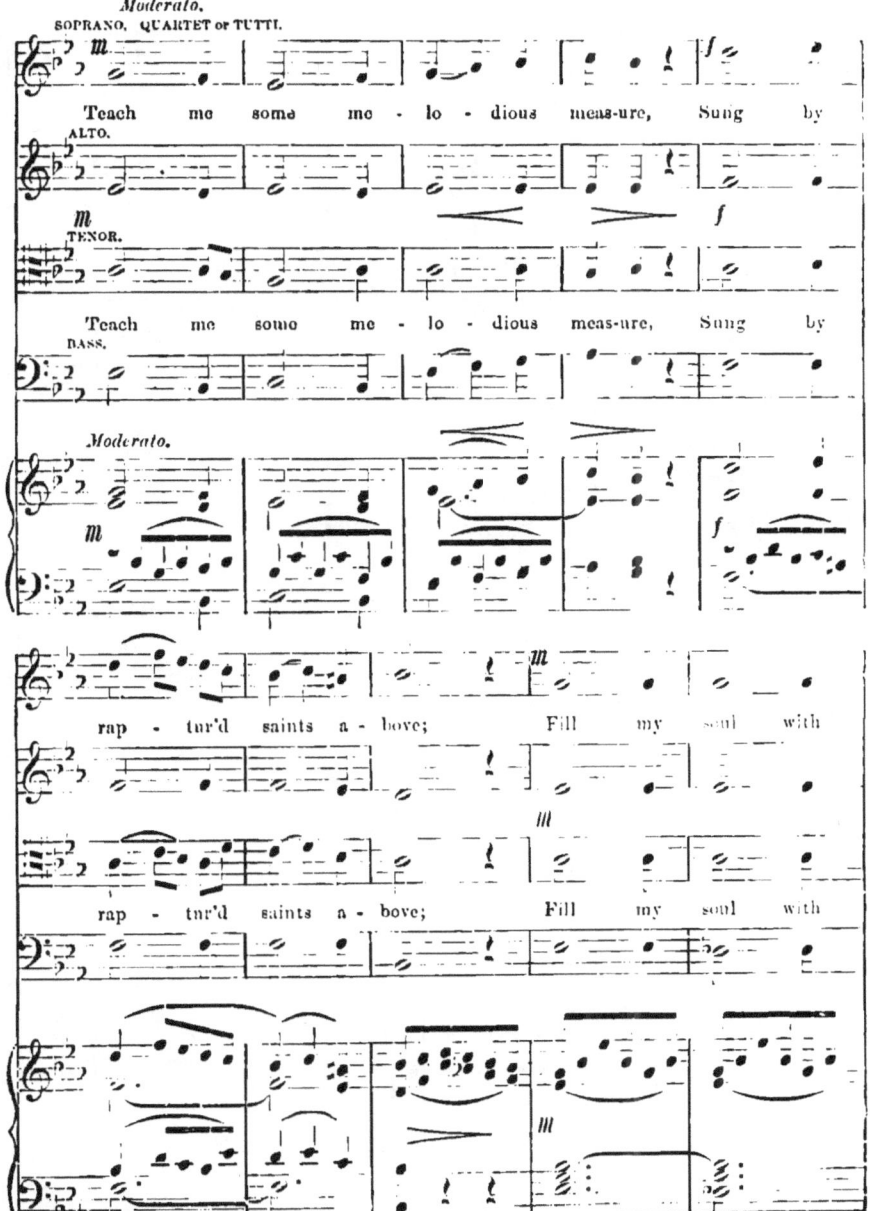

SAVIOR, SOURCE OF EV'RY BLESSING. CONTINUED.

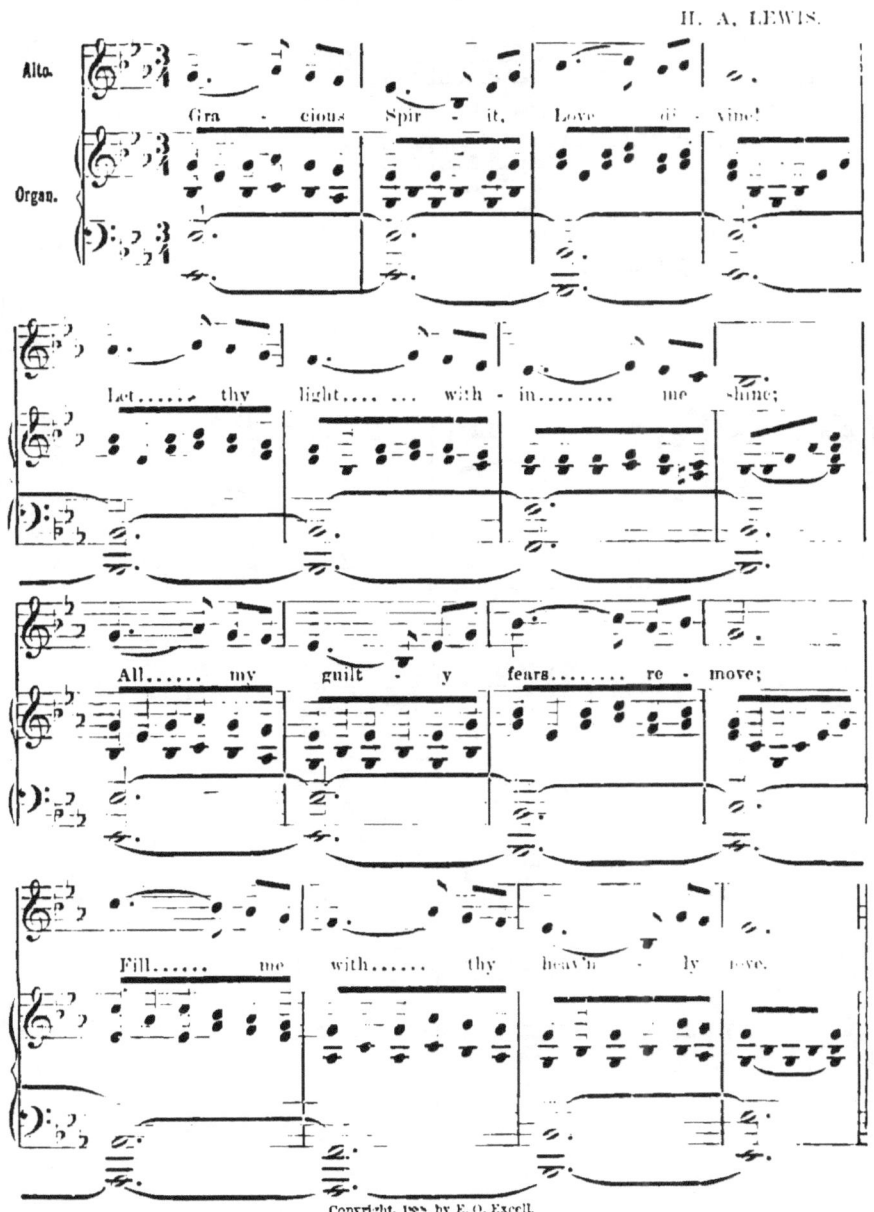

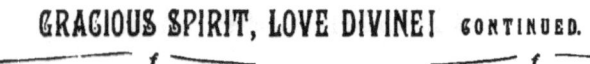

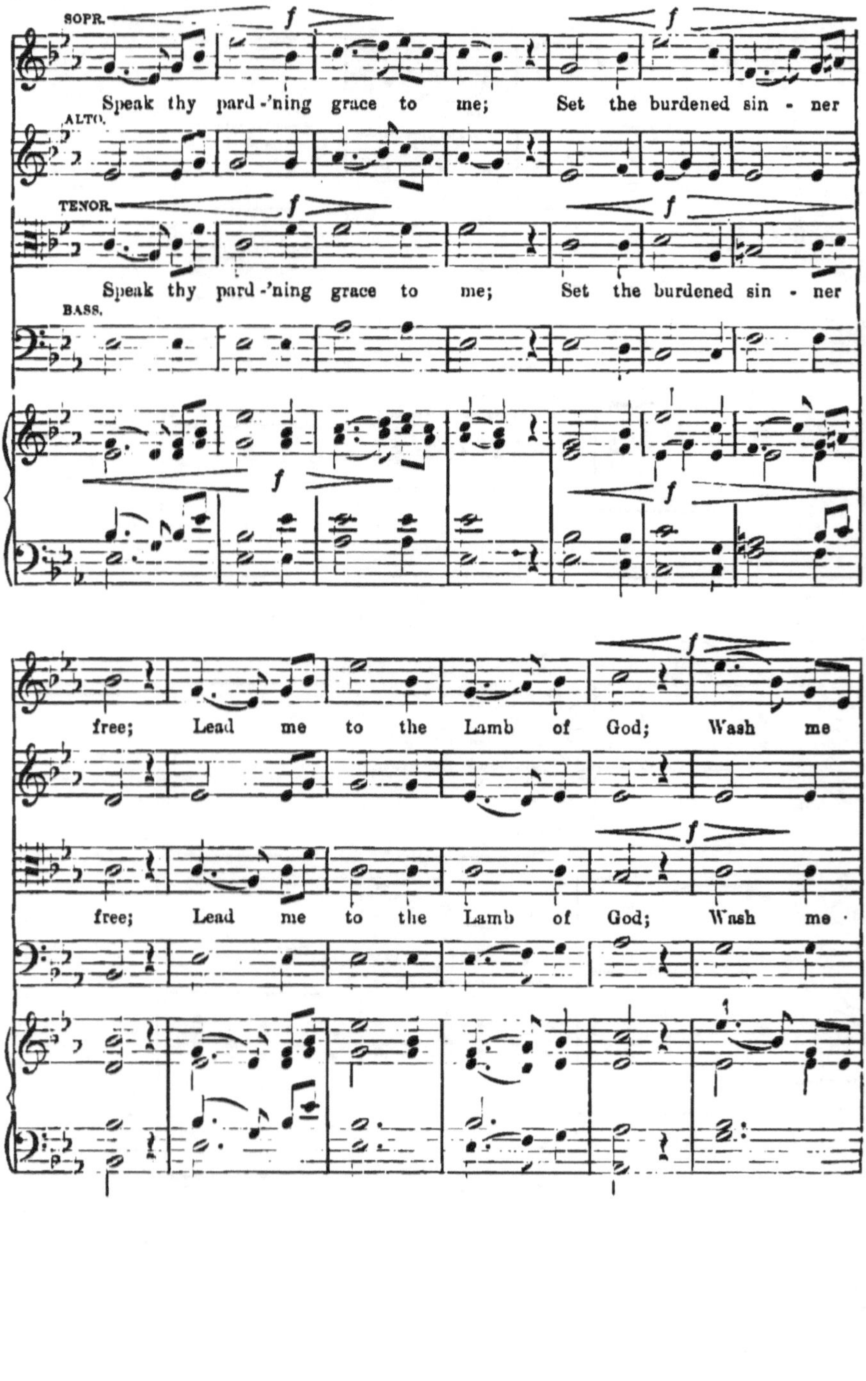
SOPR.
ALTO.
TENOR.
BASS.
f
Speak thy pard-'ning grace to me; Set the burdened sin - ner
free; Lead me to the Lamb of God; Wash me

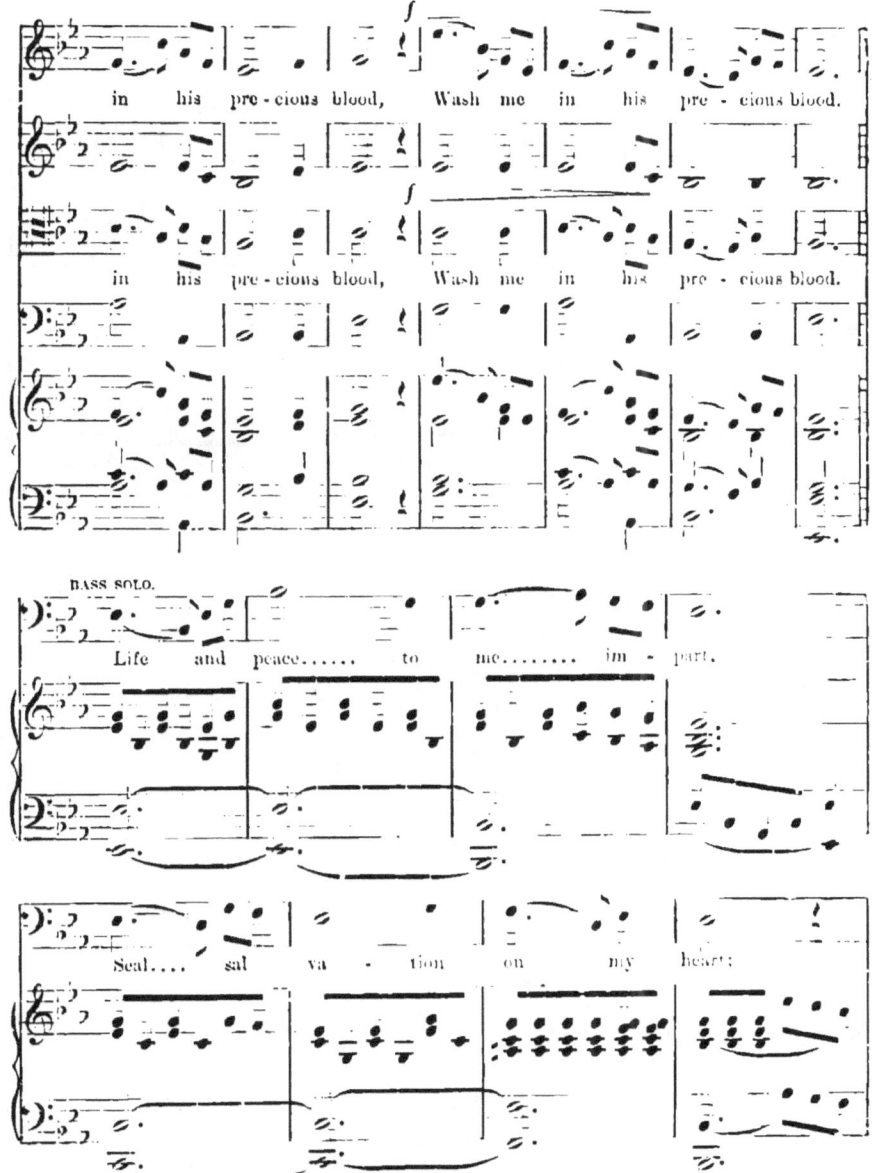

WAKE THE SONG OF JUBILEE. CONTINUED.

216 WAKE THE SONG OF JUBILEE. CONCLUDED.

LIFT UP YOUR HEADS, O YE GATES!

W. A. OGDEN.

Copyright, 1888, by E. O. Excell.

LIFT UP YOUR HEADS, O YE GATES! CONTINUED.

I WAS GLAD.

J. M. DUNGAN.

I WAS GLAD. CONTINUED.

223

PRAISE THE LORD, O JERUSALEM. CONTINUED.

rall.
Who is a - ble to a - bide his frost?
colla voce.
A tempo.
m cres. poco a poco.
He send - eth out his word and melt - eth them, He
m cres.
He send - eth out his word and melt - eth them, He
A tempo. cres. poco a poco.
m

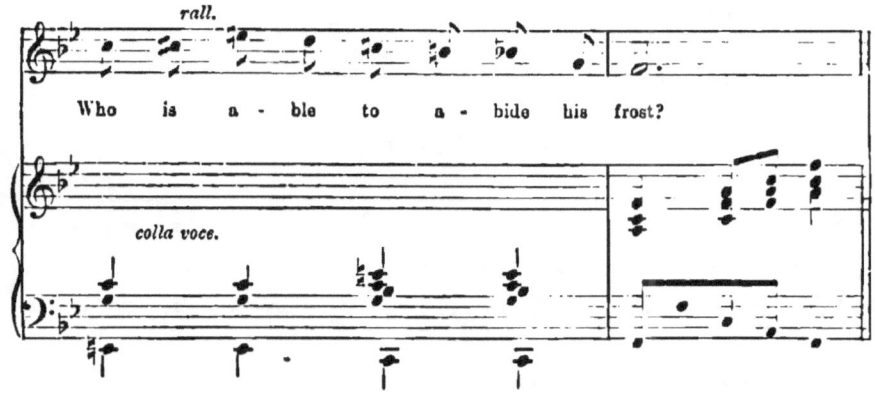

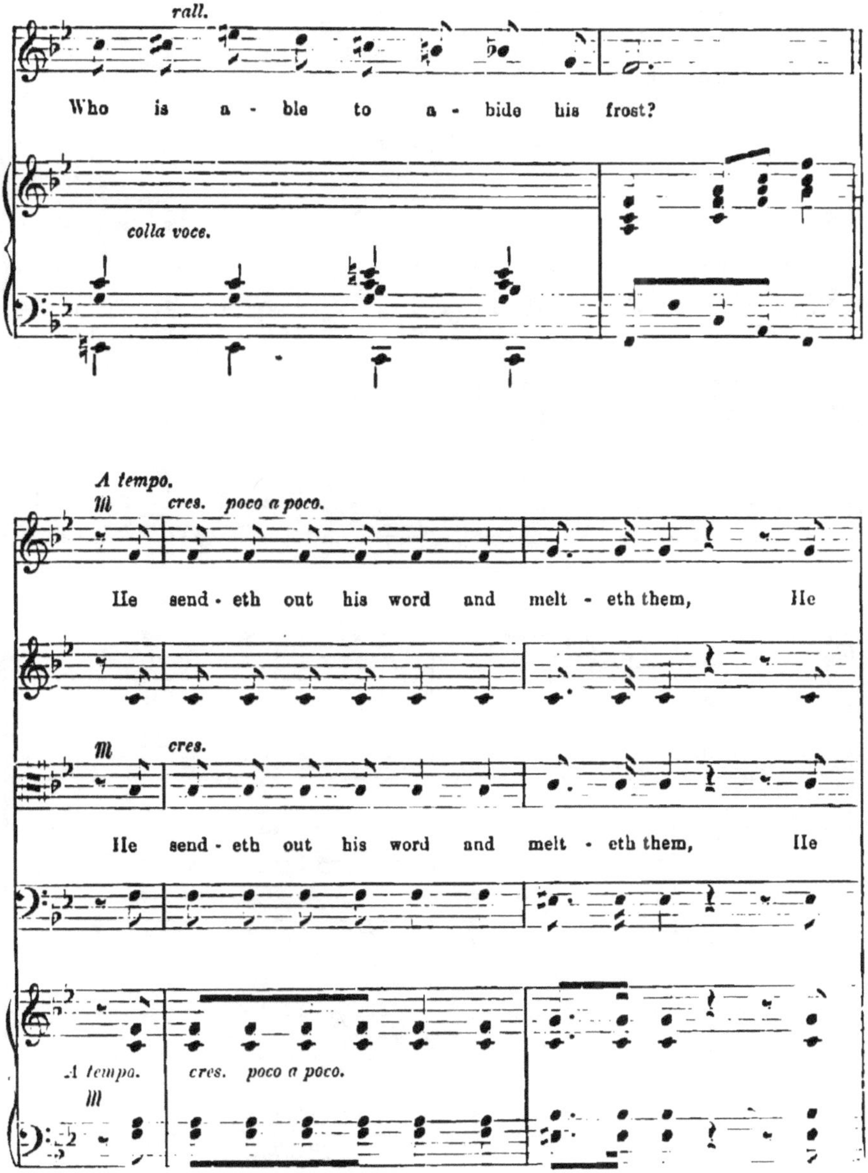

PRAISE THE LORD, O JERUSALEM. CONCLUDED.

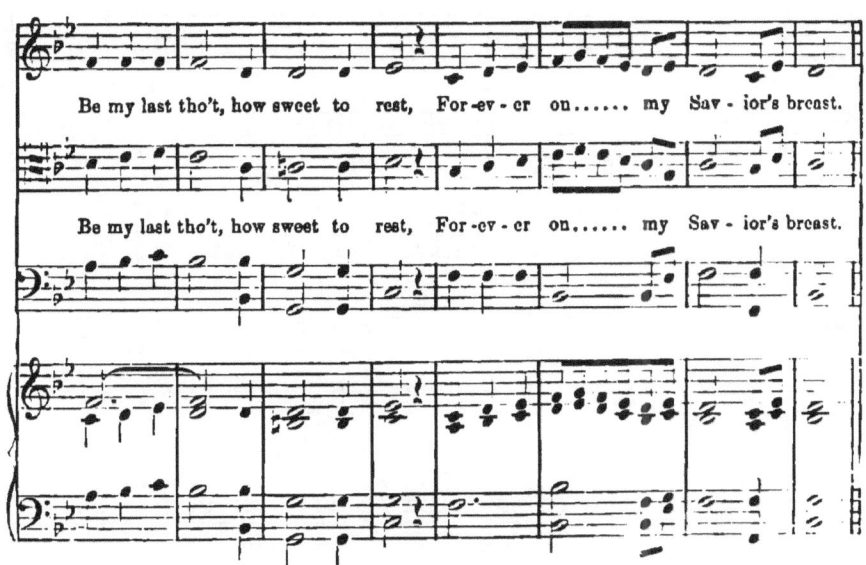

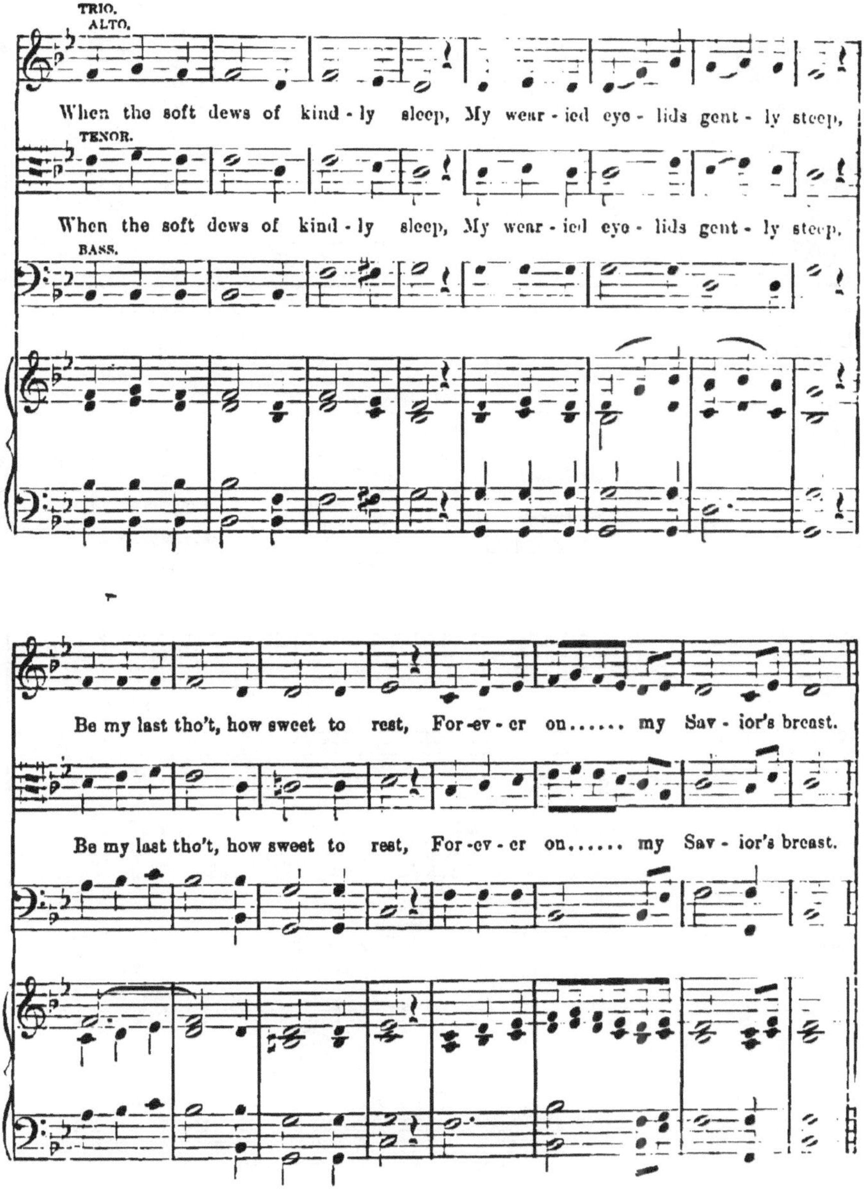
TRIO.
ALTO.
When the soft dews of kind - ly sleep, My wear - ied eye - lids gent - ly steep,
TENOR.
When the soft dews of kind - ly sleep, My wear - ied eye - lids gent - ly steep,
BASS.
Be my last tho't, how sweet to rest, For - ev - er on...... my Sav - ior's breast.
Be my last tho't, how sweet to rest, For - ev - er on...... my Sav - ior's breast.

I WILL LIFT UP MINE EYES. CONTINUED.

I WILL LIFT UP MINE EYES. CONTINUED.

244 I WILL LIFT UP MINE EYES. CONTINUED.

AS PANTETH THE HART.

FRANK M. DAVIS.

Copyright, 1888, by E. O. Excell.

AS PANTETH THE HART. CONTINUED. 247

THE LORD IS MERCIFUL.

CLARA H. SCOTT.

Copyright, 1888, by E. O. Excell.

HE GIVETH HIS BELOVED SLEEP. CONCLUDED.

While the tem - - pest still is high;
Still sup - port and com - - fort me.
Heal the sick, and lead the blind.
m
QUARTETTE or CHORUS.
m
SOPRANO.
Hide me, O,............. my Sav - - ior,
All my trust.......... on thee is
Just and ho - - ly is thy
ALTO.
Hide me, O, my Sav - ior, hide,
All my trust on thee is stay'd,
Just and ho - ly is thy name,
TENOR.
m
BASS.
m

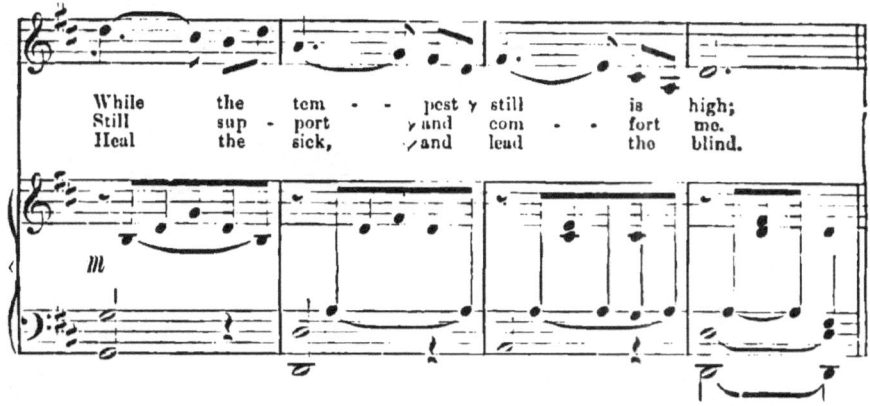

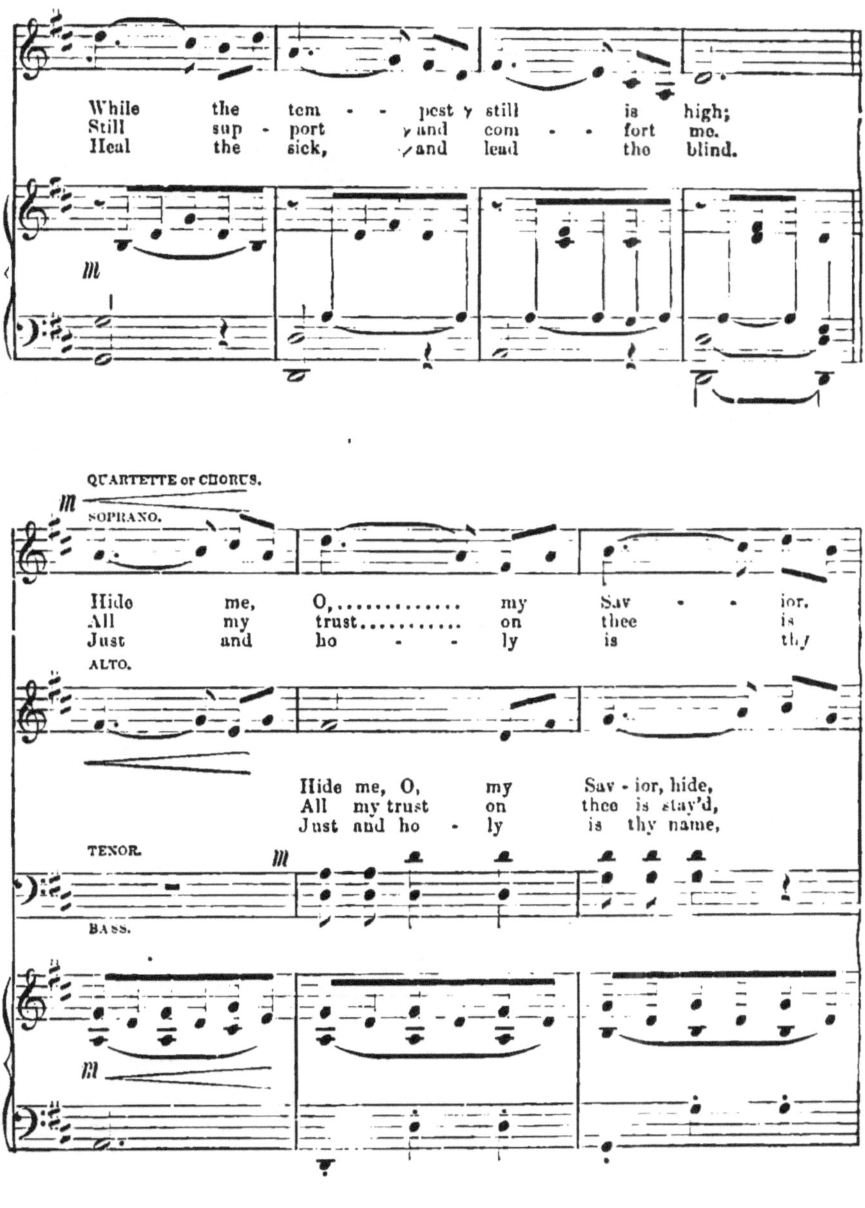

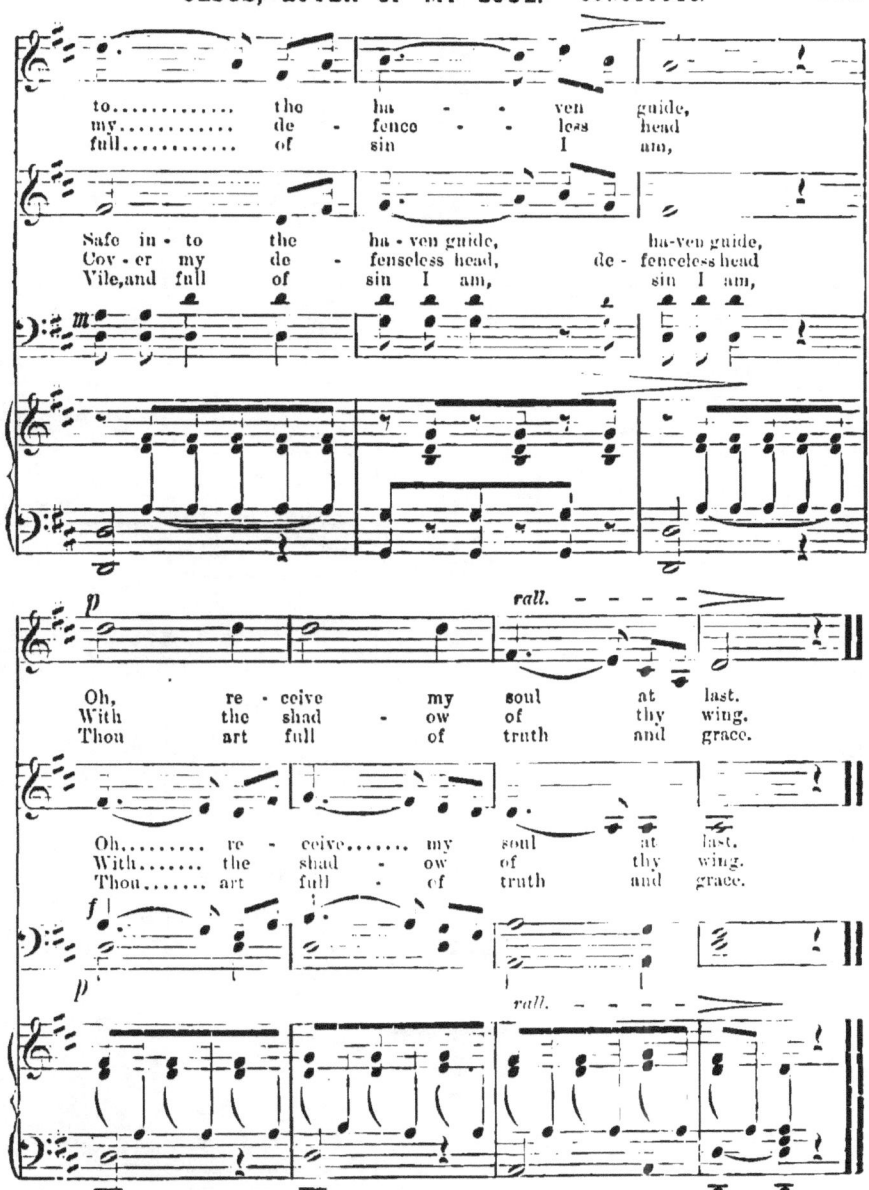

TRUST IN THE LORD AND DO GOOD. CONTINUED.

TRUST IN THE LORD AND DO GOOD. CONCLUDED.

I WILL PRAISE THEE.

E. T. O'KANE.

Copyright, 1888, by E. O. Excell.

I WILL PRAISE THEE. CONTINUED. 283

O BE JOYFUL.

H. W. FAIRBANK.

By permission.

O BE JOYFUL. CONTINUED.

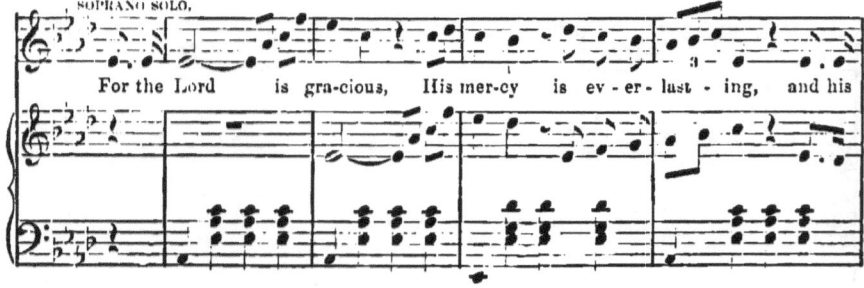

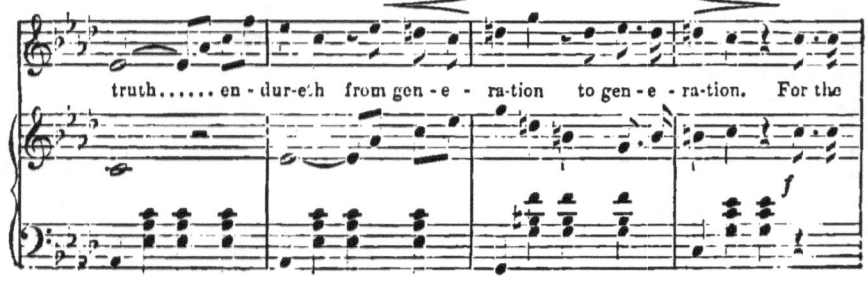

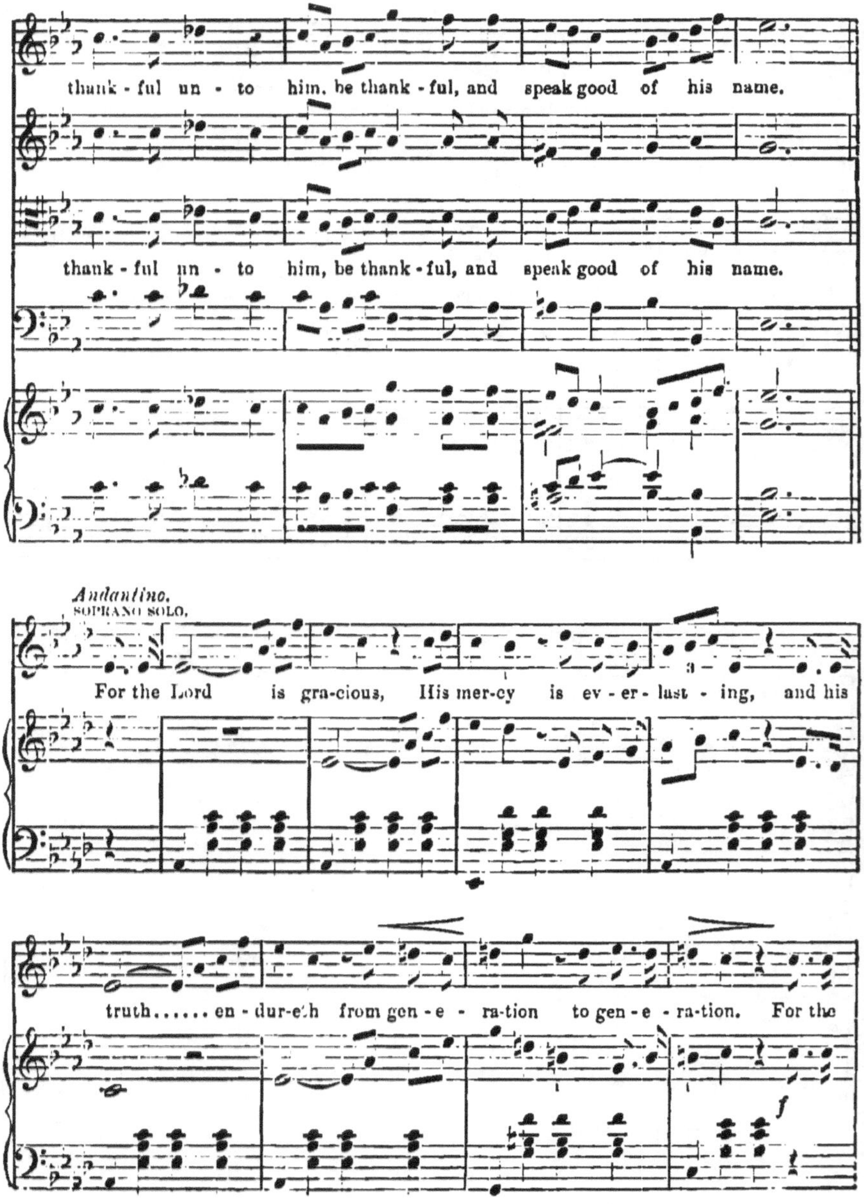
thank - ful un - to him, be thank - ful, and speak good of his name.
thank - ful un - to him, be thank - ful, and speak good of his name.
Andantino.
SOPRANO SOLO.
For the Lord is gra-cious, His mer-cy is ev - er - last - ing, and his
truth...... en - dur-eth from gen - e - ra-tion to gen - e - ra-tion. For the
f

O BE JOYFUL. CONTINUED. 291

O BE JOYFUL. CONCLUDED.

294. DEPARTED FRIENDS.

GEO. H. RYDER.

1. Weep no more for friends departed, Nor despair with grief forlorn;
2. There are loving hearts to cherish, There are those who need our cheer.
3. For the joys of earth are brighter, Than all doubting mortals know,

But press onward firm, true-hearted; Watch for
Let your heart go out in kindness, To the
And the woes of earth seem lighter, If to

Copyright, 1888, by E. O. Excell.

DEPARTED FRIENDS. CONCLUDED.

There we'll dwell no more in sor-row, But we'll wait our time to come;

For it soon will be to-mor-row, And we'll safe-ly rest at home.

PRAISE YE THE LORD. CONTINUED.

PRAISE YE THE LORD. CONCLUDED.

COME THOU FOUNT.

ANNIE HARRISON.
Arr. by E. O. EXCELL.

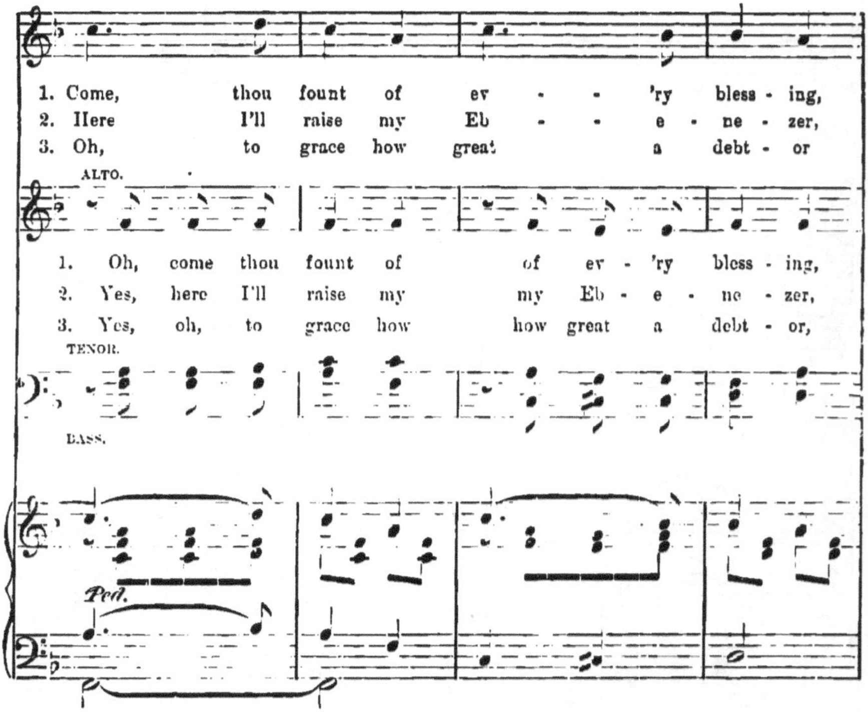

1. Come, thou fount of ev - - 'ry bless-ing,
2. Here I'll raise my Eb - - e - ne - zer,
3. Oh, to grace how great a debt - or

1. Oh, come thou fount of of ev-'ry bless-ing,
2. Yes, here I'll raise my my Eb- e - ne - zer,
3. Yes, oh, to grace how how great a debt - or,

Copyright, 1899, by E. O. Excell.

Call for songs of loud - - est praise;
Safe - ly to ar rive at home;
Bind my wand - 'ring heart to thee;
They call for songs of of loud - est praise;
Yes, safe - ly to ar ar - rive at home;
Yes, bind my wand - 'ring my heart to thee;

SOLO.
Teach me some me - lo - dious son - net Sung by flaming tongues a - bove,
Je - sus sought me when a stran - ger, Wand - 'ring from the fold of God,
Prone to wan - der Lord, I feel it, Prone to leave the God I lo
p

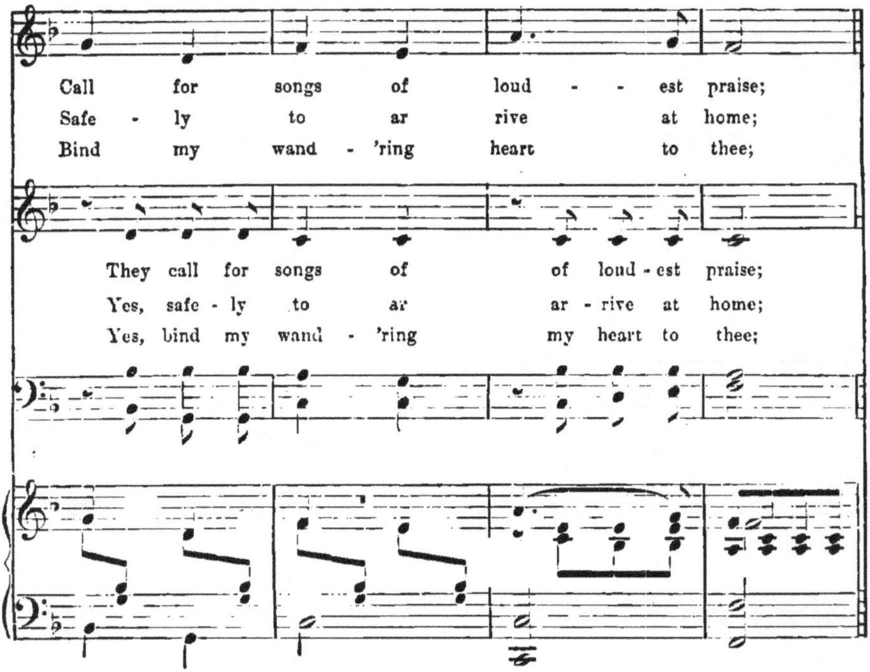

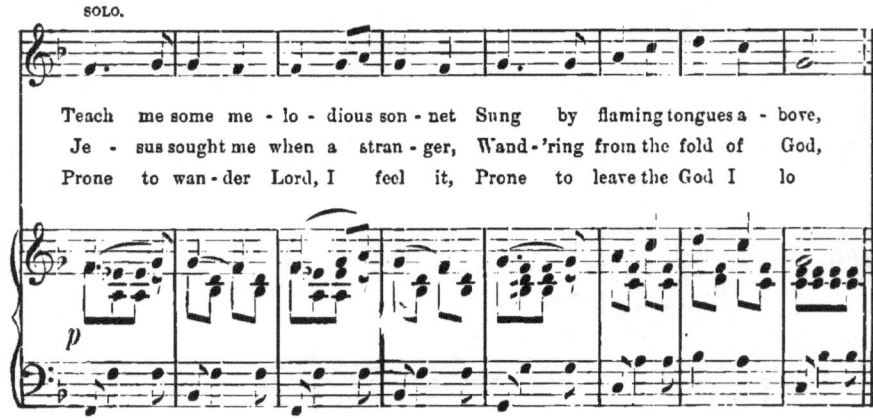

THE NATIONS WHO ARE SAVED.

WHITTINGTON.
Arr. by W. A. OGDEN.

Copyright, 1889, by E. O. Excell.

GLORY TO GOD IN THE HIGHEST.

H. P. DANKS.

Copyright, 1888, by E. O. Excell.

GLORY TO GOD IN THE HIGHEST. CONTINUED.

GLORY TO GOD IN THE HIGHEST. CONTINUED.

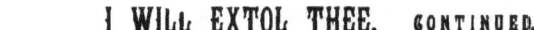

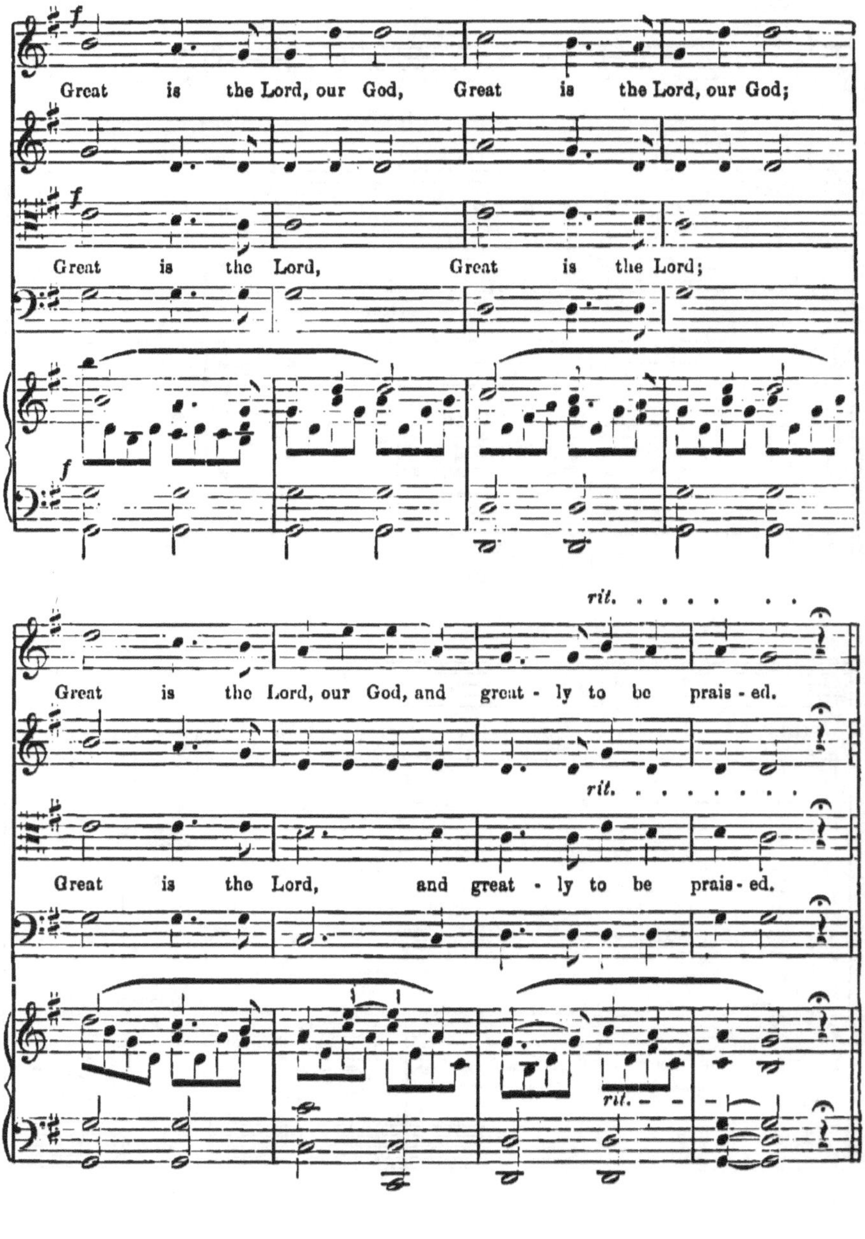
f
Great is the Lord, our God, Great is the Lord, our God;
Great is the Lord, Great is the Lord;
rit.
Great is the Lord, our God, and great - ly to be prais - ed.
rit.
Great is the Lord, and great - ly to be prais - ed.
rit.

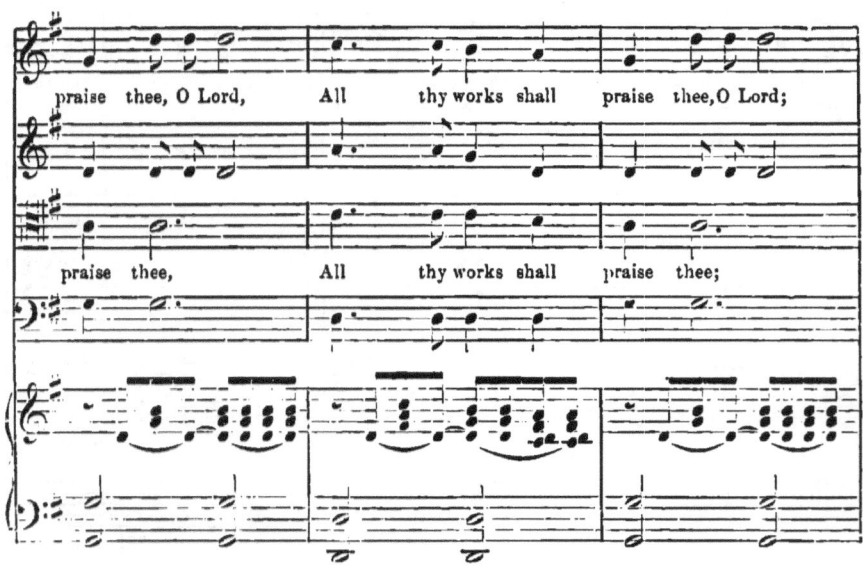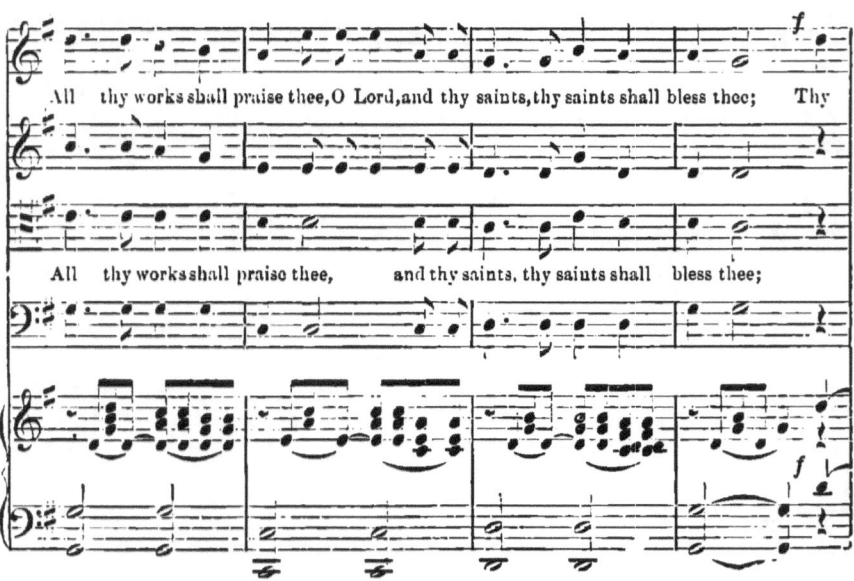

328. THERE IS A FOUNTAIN FILL'D WITH BLOOD.

A. BEIRLY.

Copyright, 1888, by E. O. Excell.

334. HEARKEN, O LORD.

MACKENZIE.
Arr. by W. A. O.

Heark-en, O Lord, to my pe-ti-tion, And in-cline thine ear, In-

cline thine ear, O Lord, O Lord, Speed-i-ly make

Copyright, 1888, by E. O. Excell.

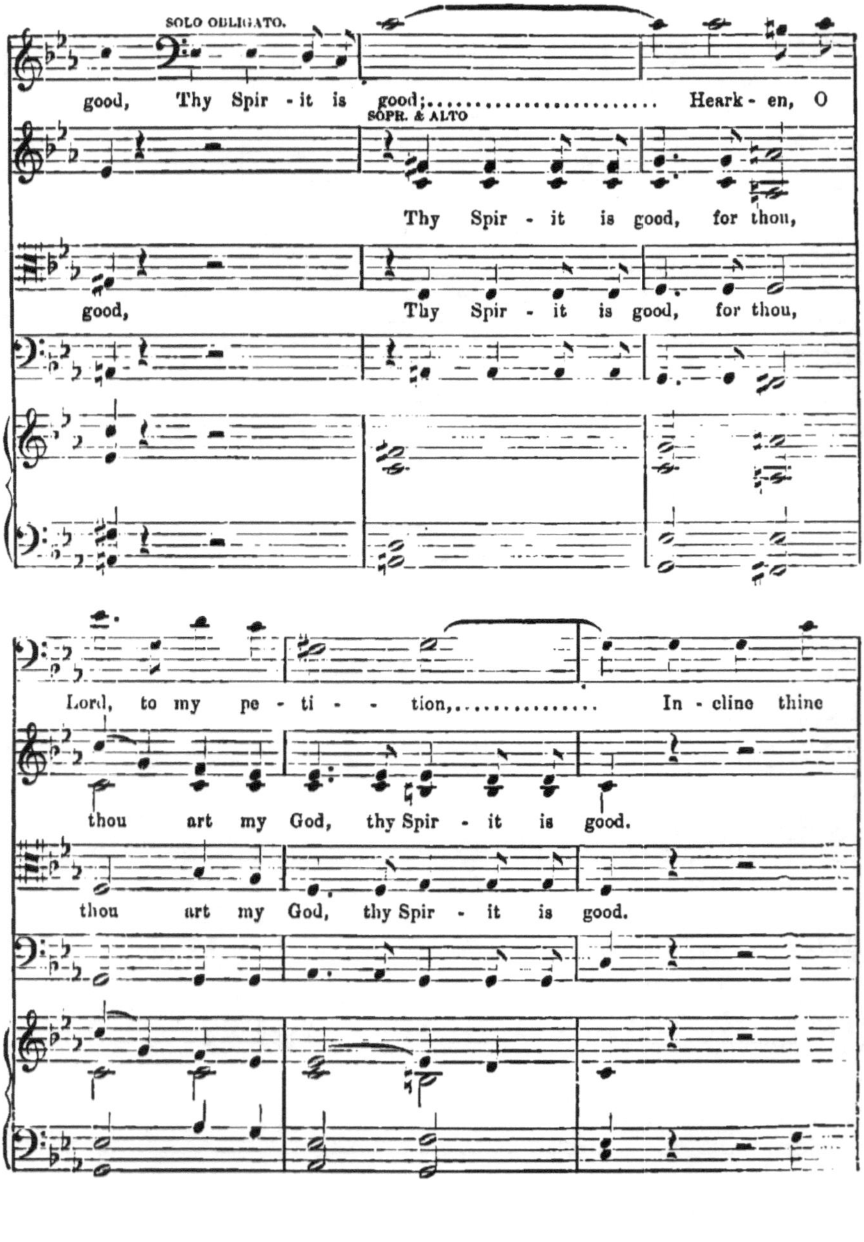
SOLO OBLIGATO.
good, Thy Spir - it is good;........................ Heark - en, O
SOPR. & ALTO
Thy Spir - it is good, for thou,
good, Thy Spir - it is good, for thou,
Lord, to my pe - ti - - tion,............... In - cline thine
thou art my God, thy Spir - it is good.
thou art my God, thy Spir - it is good.

COME, HOLY SPIRIT.

A. BEIRLY.

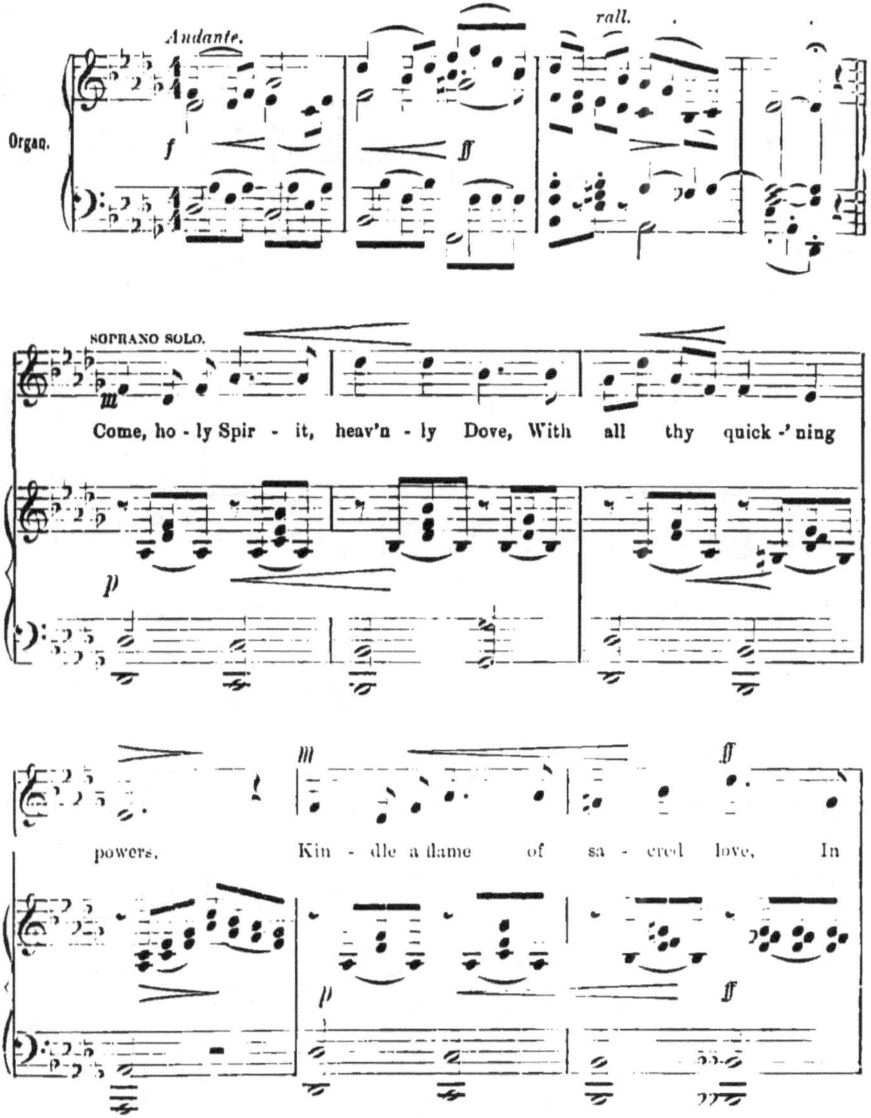
Andante.
rall.
Organ.
f
ff
SOPRANO SOLO.
mf
Come, ho - ly Spir - it, heav'n - ly Dove, With all thy quick -'ning
p
powers, Kin - dle a flame of sa - cred love, In
mf
ff
p
ff

344 COME, HOLY SPIRIT. CONTINUED.

vo- tion dies; Hosannas languish on......... our tongues, And our devotion dies, And our devotion dies.

348. O PRAISE THE LORD.

JOHN R. SWENEY.

O PRAISE THE LORD. CONTINUED.

O PRAISE THE LORD. CONTINUED.

ONE SWEETLY SOLEMN THOUGHT. CONTINUED. 357

ONE SWEETLY SOLEMN THOUGHT. CONCLUDED. 359